I WON'T be SILENT

A Memoir of Abuse, written By

ANONYMOUS JANE

Anonymous Jane

Copyright © 2025 by Anonymous Jane

All rights reserved.

No part of this publication may be reproduced, distributed, or transmitted in any form or by any means, including photocopying, recording, or other electronic or mechanical methods, without the prior written permission of the publisher, except as permitted by U.S. copyright law. For permission requests, contact Anonymous Jane.

For privacy reasons, some names and dates may have been changed.

ALL events written in this memoir are based on real interactions that occurred.

Book Cover & photos by Anonymous Jane

3rd edition, 2025

"Blessed are ye, when men shall revile you, and persecute you, and shall say all manner of evil against you falsely, for my sake."

Matthew 5:11 KJV

"For every one that doeth evil hateth the light, neither cometh to the light, lest his deeds should be reproved."

John 3:20 KJV

Table of Contents

Preface 7
Chapter One 14
Chapter Two 23
Chapter Three 28
"The Incident" 43
"Patterns" 49
Chapter Four 71
Chapter Five 83
Chapter Six 104
Conclusion 112
Epilogue 117
Dedications 125

Preface

People always say: ***"Your high school years, are your best years."*** But for me, it was a journey through hell that scarred my mind and ruined my reputation and reality with false accusations and torment. To the curious *reader(s)* who choose to peruse my memoir, hello, I'm **Anonymous Jane**. My name is of no importance, but I am a survivor of verbal abuse, slander, sexualization, psychological torment and sexual harassment from students, teachers, and faculty at the now defunct, **St. Joseph's (All-Girls) High School in Brooklyn, New York (80 Willoughby St, 11201).**

Throughout those agonizing four years, my reputation was ruined, the students would hurl insults at me, even in the middle of class to laugh and humiliate me in unison, defame me as being promiscuous, falsely accuse me of seducing the teachers, call me homophobic and transphobic slurs to mock my appearance and egregiously dehumanize me due to my quiet nature and avoidance of them.

Eventually, the teachers, both male and female, young and old, would mimic the students' behaviors, either subtly or conspicuously, while hypocritically calling themselves *"progressive"* and *"inclusive"*. The repulsive instructors were the epitome of demons in human skin.

I'm aware the logical solution was to transfer to another school. But, due to my previous experience of being slandered and tormented in jr. high, I was *cynical and depressed* that I would be harassed if I were to attend a different school.

I'm willing to bet, if I told some individuals the defamation and harassment I experienced in high school, they would spout a generic banality like: *"It gets better"*. In turn, I would reveal that I have been sexually harassed and falsely persecuted from junior high, the neighborhood I moved into as a minor, high school and college.

"So, when does it get better?"

Sometimes, I wonder if the devil is the one that machinated my misfortune, like *Job*, or were the institutions I chose, were filled with malicious, dysgenic people, like *Nineveh, Sodom and Gomorrah*. It's possible that both can be true.

Even as an adult, those memories of being mistreated, slandered and tormented run through my mind *like acid expanding and corroding on a fresh, bloody, wound.* For this memoir, I'll unveil the abuse I endured from **shithole SJHS**.

I still remember overhearing the backbiting school guidance counselor, calling me a *"future prostitute"* under her rancid breath, after I finished the final standardized test. I still reminisce about the perverted vice-principal blaming me for my body and hurling sexual insults at me. Even to this day, I still remember the repulsive female shrews who sexually harassed me for their perverse enjoyment.

Out of all the torment I experienced, I was left with anxiety attacks, flashbacks, meltdowns, bouts of anger and regret. My mind would subconsciously reminisce those horrible memories and I would undergo feelings of anger and regret, wishing I was bit more violent. In worse situations, I have suffered meltdowns where I burst into tears due to multiple cretins sexually harassing me and defaming my reputation.

In adulthood, these scars haven't healed and persist to this day.

The moment I first entered **shithole SJHS,** I could tell I was going to be harassed and bullied. Most of the teenagers were loud, pushy, spouted sex jokes. As for the instructors and faculty, their demeanors and behaviors unraveled as the semesters continued.

On the first day of Freshman year, I kept repeating statements in my head that conveyed how the raucous, uncouth students and shady instructors would treat me for the next four years. Eventually, these predictions came true.

"I am going to be bullied here."

"The teachers are going to berate me."

"The students will slander me for their own enjoyment."

"These demons here will feed on my misery."

"I... just want to be left alone."

"I don't want any attention."

"They'll misunderstand me, for my body."

While you, *dear reader,* may assume I was **"too negative"** or call this a self-fulfilled prophecy. The fact that the pedagogy and student body's eventual mistreatment towards me was *detected*(intuitively) *early*, is evident that their true nature is equivalent to **savages.**

I don't desire any notoriety from my experiences, I only intend to expose the ***true character*** of these slanderous, abusive, sanctimonious, "Christian" instructors. Furthermore, I'm writing this memoir because throughout most of my life, I've always felt powerless. I was born and raised in poverty, and authority figures never took me or my distress seriously since I am and was, quiet, unpopular, depressed, asocial and neurodivergent. If the vile instructors and students were aware of my neurodivergence, they would've harassed and castigated me even more.

But not anymore. *I don't care if I have no power or social status, I can't let the truth die.*

I won't be silent anymore.

To this day, I believe there are multiple causes for my abuse, slander being one of them, but most importantly, due to my appearance. From junior high onwards, I was an *early bloomer*, my body was maturing, my hips were growing which made me even more self-conscious, and I only desired to be invisible throughout my school life.

Furthermore, ***I was a loner by choice,*** who refused to acclimate the crude and boisterous **snakes**(students) and their hypocritical behaviors. Likewise, since shithole SJHS was a Catholic school, I bet the uptight, self-righteous teachers automatically assumed my body was *"sinful"* and most likely believed the bestial students' slander.

Another reason might be racial, since I was a shy, black girl, opposite of the boisterous, belligerent, confrontational, argumentative stereotype. Maybe, my quiet personality gave them the reason to harass me, along with spreading baseless rumors. Third, the female teachers were probably envious and the male instructors, couldn't control themselves.

Evidently, these charlatans possess no morality, especially Christian values. Their maltreatment magnified my unshakeable sense of justice and so I've taken it upon myself to unveil the vile pedagogues of shithole SJHS, their disgusting nature and their sadistic tendencies.

As for crudely mocking and describing all the pedo-adjacent pedagogues, is the most apropos descriptors for them.

These worthless excuses for teachers don't deserve any *tact* or *respect* from me. Subsequently, the cruelty and slander that they revealed to me shows they can't respect themselves, either and are poor role models. It's thanks to them, I experienced how "evil" disguises itself as "good".

In no specific order, these are the teachers who slandered and verbally abused me:

Sister Barabbas(principal), Mr. Cain(vice-principal), Mrs. Delilah & Ms. Salome (guidance counselors), Ms. Rotten(secretary), and finally the teachers: Mr. Judas, Mr. David, Ms. Amelia, Mrs. Ramses, Mrs. Samantha, Mrs. Corpse Hag, Ms. Suzie, Mr. Measly, Mrs. Bonny and Mr. Ryan.

In this memoir, the truth, I will expose how each of these sleazebags mistreated and disparaged me.

Chapter One
Mr. Cain: Vice Principal

Starting out in St. Joseph's High School, this perverted, repugnant, ghoul was the earliest harasser I've dealt with. Adding to the fact, he was the first *"authority figure"* to start berating me. Although we rarely meet, he had the tendency to mutter or yell an insult whenever I was in his vicinity. It was loud enough for me and even others to hear, and I noticed he intended to slander me while talking to another failed excuse of an instructor, or when he walked past me.

This disgusting, decrepit, shambling, corpse (that I dub **"Sleazy-C"**) would always call me a *"fat-ass hoe"* due to my curvy body, in his baseless delusion of me trying to seduce him. Sleazy-C's beratement towards me was a mirror of the abuse I faced in jr. high. *As a youth, I knew I couldn't help the fact that my body was shapely, and I already had body image issues. Why did these dim-witted instructors judge me based on my appearance?*

Sleazy-C's harassment towards me began in the early autumn of my freshman year. The first incident occurred at dismissal, when I was walking in the hallway alone. I was leaving a school club, and he was behind me. He kept muttering:

"C'mon, I don't want you.",

falsely accusing me of trying to seduce him, even though I did nothing to him. At the time I was very hyper-vigilant and worried over the way I walked. My maturing body made my prominent hips sway, which resulted in the psychological torture I experienced in Jr. high.

To add insult to injury, I was left with even more self-hatred over my body issues. From my perspective, since I predicted that I would be harassed again by observing the instructors' behaviors, they really undermined theirs, especially Mr. Cain's competence and emotional intelligence at their professions.

Another verbal harassment incident happened during Sophomore year. Shortly after the semester began, early September, my class schedule was disorganized, and I had to report to Sleazy-C's office to receive a new one. He appeared courteous when we talked face to face. But, after some time I arrived at the library, he entered, and while conversing with the librarian, I overheard him say:

"That fat-ass hoe was trying to act all cutesy while I gave her the schedule."

I never did anything to him, except be courteous and respectful to an adult, as I was raised to be. I felt pangs of disgust, bitterness, and righteous indignation that worthless pile of dung would falsely accuse me, as well as see me in a sexual manner.

In mid-October of the same year, I remember all Freshmen, Sophomore students and their respective teachers all assembled in the gymnasium. The occasion was called the *"Walk-a-thon"*, where everyone walked across the Brooklyn bridge, then returned. While I was walking around trying to find my group, I walked past Sleazy-C, and he replied with:

"I don't want you, Fat-ass hoe".

That repulsive, pedo-pervert sexually harassed me, and it triggered an anxiety attack. My heart started beating rapidly; I began inhaling in short breaths. That verbal abuse attack reminded me of the same unjustified abuse I endured in jr. high. While everyone was in high spirits, I was in a state of confusion, anger, and nervousness.

Within the month April, middle of Junior Year, a celebration where all teachers as well as faculty members were to be nominated and congratulated with awards was held in **The Oratory of St. Boniface's Church**, which was adjacent to shithole SJHS.

After the ceremony, that jaded me and made me internally wretch, all the students were finally ready to line up to leave the church. When I waited in line, I noticed Sleazy-C holding a bouquet of flowers (undeservedly) and approaching another student. This student was short, either Freshman or Sophomore (both grades wore the same uniform colors: burgundy polo shirt & gray skirt/pants), looked white/white-Hispanic, had long brown, straight hair, brown eyes, and pale skin.

While the younger student was three people ahead of me, I was aware of Sleazy-C whispering something in the girl's ear and he then kissed her on the cheek.

In all my life, I've never seen a vice-principal act so brazenly and inappropriately towards a student. Plus, Sleazy-C never acted affectionately towards any other student, so, God only knows what kind of sickening connection him and the young student had.

Considering I was unjustifiably mistreated by the rest of the faculty, there's no way the vile pedagogues would believe me if I reported Sleazy-C to them. However, that repulsive incident that occurred in the church (ironically) solidified my assertations of Sleazy-C's sexual deviance and hypocrisy, just like the actual Catholic diocese.

Once again, in Junior year, in the beginning of May, during gym class, when he and two male custodians were walking by the whole class and me, exercising, I overheard him saying:

"I don't want you, fat-ass, hoe."

Sleazy-C couldn't control himself and decided to sexually harass me, once again. I loathed this filthy pervert from the bottom of my heart.

As for Senior year, on Orientation day, my classmates and I were sitting at separate tables, where I preferably sat alone. As Sleazy-C walked by and conversed with some of the other snakes, I overheard my slanderous would-be classmates saying to him:

"She [Jane] wants you…She wants you…"

and he would reply: ***"I don't want her."***

Thus, both the snakes and Sleazy-C would continue to spread rumors about me seducing the teachers with my body, working together by demeaning my character. Forming the self-proclaimed pious institute, a den of liars, and pigs.

Finally, the last time I heard him utter more verbal abuse towards me was also in my Senior year.

It was primary to mid-April, early one morning, I was walking towards the elevators to head to homeroom, when Sleazy-C and a snake named, **Zoe**, were talking amongst each other on the staircase. The moment I walked by them; he hurled the phrase towards me:

"Quiet Turd."

Zoe, one of the "smart" students, proceeded to laugh along with Sleazy-C's harassment of me.

This disgusting sleazebag generated another internal anxiety attack at that moment, and part of me wanted to scream at him.

Ultimately, this vile excuse of an administrator, ***now turned priest*** is very apropos for demonstrating an incorrigible, perverted, borderline-pedophilic behavior, that is a walking disgrace to God, Jesus, and the Holy Spirit.

Whatever ranks Sleazy-C, the walking bag of excrement, ascends to in the Catholic Church is inconsequential since hell awaits those who abuse & slander minors.

Chapter Two
Mrs. Corpse Hag: Arts and Crafts Teacher

If there was ever an envious, slanderous, pallid, ***skeleton***, that was unnecessarily *vitriolic* towards me, it was her: Mrs. **"Crazy Corpse Hag Cunt"** *(Corpse Hag for short)*, as I like to call her. Being the wife of the depraved, Sleazy-C, it was evident she believed those baseless rumors and even verbally abused me(subtly). Unlike Sleazy-C, this so-called feminist, would hurl insults as well as threats of violence under her rotten slug of a tongue and decaying green pebbles for teeth. At the time, I was naively expecting her to converse rationally if she had any problems with me.

But if this corpse hag was stupid enough to call me a "whore" because of my curvy physique and falsely accuse me seducing her chimo husband then it's obvious she lacks wisdom and intelligence beyond arts and crafts.

My first beratement from the Corpse Hag was in Sophomore year, in the earlier months (around autumn) of the semester.

All I did was enter the art room, grab my supplies from the shelf and right before I sat down, I heard…

"I wish I can choke [JANE]." The Corpse Hag hissed with venom.

She ***psychopathically,*** blatantly and calmly described her murderous intent to Mrs. Gums, another arts teacher, who was her best friend, and laughed along with her. Right after her threat of violence, the Corpse Hag conspicuously snarled & remarked:

"You can tell [Jane] is a whore."

At the time, I fell into a state of shock, my body began to quiver, my heart was pounding across my chest, and my breathing was more rapid. At that moment, when I heard this, I attempted to stay calm and quietly did my work.

But I loathed the environment I was in, and realized my prediction came true. I had a feeling the Corpse Hag would end up as one of my *enemies* due to her lack of morals and baseless rumors spread about me.

Looking back at this moment, not only did she slander me, but she also displayed her racist tendencies in assuming I, a Black female minor was a prostitute for being buxom and lying about me bewitching her ***decrepit, rotten, borderline pedophile*** of a husband.

Even though the Corpse Hag stopped spouting blatant lies and threats, I always detected a sense of inappropriate animosity and hostility whenever she conversed with me.

In junior year, I caught the Corpse Hag defaming my character, one winter morning, I chose to relax in the library during a free period. As I was signing my signature into the library attendance sheet, the wretched, mendacious, Corpse Hag was conversing with a young adult, white woman who had long, curly, blond hair, blue eyes and was wearing a long black dress. The woman gave the impression she was a *visiting student teacher*, since she was holding bright colored books meant for a children's classroom.

I ignored most of the conversation between the Corpse Hag and the female teacher, but I noticed when the hag indirectly mentioned me in a falsity. From my peripheral view, the corpse hag, pointed her gaunt, pale finger towards me and lied to the female teacher:

> *"...That's HER. She tends to write about smut and pornography."*

While I was internally enraged at the hag's false accusation about my hobby, I decided to stay calm, collected, and mature.

The female teacher reacted in disgust, believing that lie. Even though I wasn't surprised at the Corpse Hag's behavior, she gave me an insight that's she very gullible as well as a filthy liar. Among the **snakes** (student body) they all tended to falsely label me with even more ridiculous, random, and baseless lies that change every few weeks. I wouldn't be surprised if the Corpse Hag heard that groundless rumor from them. Pertaining to the snakes and lying pedagogues, slandering me was the norm for their sick enjoyment of gossip and hyperbole, indicative of *toxic femininity*.

For a **"grown"** adult feminist like the Corpse Hag to embezzle and defame an innocent student with such lies, her behavior ironically reinforces the sexist notion: of *"don't ever believe a woman's word."*

I wonder, since Sleazy-C predated on a minor female student with similar features as the Corpse Hag (same hair, skin and eye color), was she aware of her husband's degeneracy? Was there trouble in Paradise? Did Sleazy-C grow tired of her? Either way, they're both destined for hell.

Altogether, it's no surprise the wife of Sleazy-C would engage in slanderous harassment towards a minor. As all people were raised to respect teachers in our youth, **Mrs. Corpse Hag Cunt,** and the other instructors disillusioned the belief that all teaching adults deserve respect and served to be a disgrace to the teaching profession.

The next few people I'm about to expose are those who've slandered and/or harassed me **at least once**. Even though my encounters with them were minimal, I'm addressing them to showcase the fact that the lies both students and faculty spread about me showed me that shithole St. Joseph's HS was a collective hivemind of slanderers, sadists, and sexual harassers.

Chapter Three

<u>Ms. Suzie (English Teacher), Mrs. Ramses (math teacher), Ms. Rotten(secretary), Ms. Amelia (gym teacher), Mrs. Gums, Ms. Salome and Mr. Ryan</u>

Continuing the trend of repulsive, broad, **crone** instructors berating me during my tenure at SJHS, was the Sophomore math teacher Mrs. Ramses.

Even though she was African American, her slander towards me demonstrated she was subservient to the white leftist, majority instructors like a lapdog and participated in their harassment. While Mrs. Ramses was also short, old, dumpy, obese, and ugly inside and out. She had the audacity and delusion to sexually harass and falsely accuse me of trying to seduce her. The only incident she brazenly berated me was during the middle of class on an early October day, when I was minding my own business.

At the time, all the verbal abuse and bullying I underwent throughout junior high, and the previous year made me very anxious and resulted in my legs uncontrollably shaking while I sat at my desk.

On that day, Mrs. Ramses the vile predator, yelled to the whole class:

"I don't want your cooch" towards me.

I don't know how she stupidly inferred I was trying to seduce her, but the corpulent chimo slandered me, just like the other instructors. After Mrs. Ramses publicly humiliated me, the rest of the mendacious student body laughed in unison. Subsequently, the students from varying grades would spread rumors of me tempting that sycophantic, lying, disgusting, bestial predator.

Another time the vile, sexual harassing, **barbaric hippo** slandered me occurred in autumn, Sophomore year. One day, I wore blue denim pants with my burgundy blouse, since my gray khaki pants needed to be washed.

Mrs. Ramses noticed my pants (*but not the snakes showing off their lower backs*) while distributing a paper notice to the math class. She informed me I had to change into a pair of gray khakis that the school carried, in a wardrobe next to the main office.

After math class, Mrs. Ramses guided me to the office and handed me those extra pair of khakis. For the rest of the day, I had to wear them, and I felt uncomfortable.

Luckily the khakis were clean. But they were slightly large for me. Plus, the thought of someone else wearing these khakis before me made my skin crawl, since I started noticing some snakes traipsing the halls scratching at their dark, crusty and peeling necks while doused with a subtle, musty odor that follows them.

Once the day ended, I changed back to my denim pants. In my nervousness, haste, and social awkwardness, I thought I had to return the khakis to Mrs. Ramses herself. So, I stood outside her classroom, in the empty hallway, holding the pants. Regrettably, I shouldn't have stood there. After a few minutes, the barbaric hippo noticed me while she was teaching her class.

"Are you here to sell yourself?" Ramses berated me with.

The hippo's vile remark triggered another internal anxiety attack from me. Afterwards, in justified anger and haste, I threw the school khakis into the guidance counselor's waiting room and headed home.

Humorously, I unintentionally obtained a small form of revenge against Mrs. Ramses. At the end of Sophomore year, I placed the math textbook in a small closet filled with them, adjacent to the classroom. I assumed that was the appropriate action, but apparently students were supposed to hand the textbook over to Mrs. Ramses, and she was to check it on a list next to a student's name. After discovering that process, I didn't really care. I just wanted to enjoy summer vacation.

In early June, my late mother received a call from her. Mrs. Ramses inquired where I placed the math textbook. I relayed my answer to my mother and Mrs. Ramses complained that she had to go look for it. Neither of us cared about her or her predicament.

The moment I heard about it though, I imagined that disgraceful **hippo,** *sweltering and sweating like a hog,* in shithole SJHS (due to malfunctioning Air Conditioners) searching for that textbook and forced to remain there, **much longer,** before commencing her vacation.

By next year, Mrs. Ramses, the math teacher, transferred out. Was it God's punishment? Was it a miracle of God?

Another female Sophomore teacher apart of the harangue harassers was Ms. Suzie, the English teacher. I could only speculate if her friendship with Sleazy-C resulted in her involvement of slandering me, or maybe there was something between them that only God knows.

Nevertheless, she's another example of a non-white woman verbally abusing and sexually harassing another female of color, who's a minor no less. Ironically, while being a staunch "*progressive*".

The start of her beratement began on an early October day, when the class was writing down notes over a novel, my anxiety arose as Ms. Mierda (Suzie) was in proximity to my desk. I could predict she was going to harass me.

Ms. Mierda started inappropriately, seductive dancing in the corner of my eye. While her gaze matched mines she whispered:

"You like this?".

Even though the event took a few seconds, I was disgusted at her actions and **the fact** she assumed anyone would desire an ugly, chipmunk-faced skank like her. Since Ms. Mierda was friends with the snakes, it's evident she would follow suit by believing the rumors.

For some odd reason, the **hag** teachers started assuming I was a lesbian starting in Sophomore year, which I wasn't. Even if it was true, Ms. Mierda and Mrs. Ramses sexually harassed me as minor, which I'll forever call them ***pedos/pedo-adjacent***.

Ironically, those two chimo cunts sexually harassed me when I was having an internal panic attack, further damaging my mental health. Even till today, I still remember my chest tightening, out fear of being harassed by the pedagogue, right before those two publicly humiliated, slandered and sexually harassed me in the classroom. I just wanted to be left alone, unnoticed.

In the same month, the class was taking the first test of the semester. As Ms. Mierda walked across the quiet classroom to monitor the students, the moment she passed me, she muttered in a whispered, yet audible tone:

"I bet you like to lick toes" following a snide laugh.

None of the snakes reacted, but her vile insult was audible for me and adjacent students to hear.

The third harassment incident occurred at the same assembly, (Walk-a-thon) sophomore year in the gym, after Sleazy-C sexually harassed me. When the students were gathered around for the dance club to perform their routine, I was unlucky enough to be seated where manface Ms. Mierda and Sleazy-C were standing nearby.

At the time, I was really frazzled after Sleazy-C hurled an insult to my face; it triggered my anxiety, PTSD, and nervousness. At the corner of my eye, I could see both Ms. Mierda and Sleazy-C laughing at me.

I'm aware this is a stretch, but whenever I turned my head at them, they'd look away while ridiculing me and covering their mouths.

For someone as disgusting as her, I hope and pray this repulsive shrew never continues to be an educator.

While Ms. Rotten was a secretary and my interactions with her were sparse, the two incidents where she ridiculed me were enough to prove her slanderous, and *"sycophantic to evil"* nature. Just like Ramses, she was an aging, wrinkly, black hag who went out of way to participate in the harassment towards me.

The first incident was in my junior year, mid-October, the Walk-a-thon, A.K.A, the same event where Sleazy Sleazy-C and Ms. Suzie harassed me last year in the gym. I opted not to participate and was relegated to doing clerical work for the secretaries.

Afterwards, the snakes and teachers left, Ms. Rotten assigned me and another left-behind student (short, black sophomore) to fold up some extra uniforms and sheets in a cabinet right outside the main office. The moment I picked up a school blouse from the floor, from behind me, Ms. Rotten whispered to the student (about me):

"*That's why she's called a whore.*"

Just like the other teachers, the decrepit Rotten body-shamed and slandered me for my appearance. When I heard her remark and muffled laugh from the student, I had a slight panic attack because I was fearful Rotten and now that student will slander my name among the student body.

For the second incident was during the middle of my senior year, where I went to the office for volunteer work. As I sat there on a waiting bench, Ms. Rotten, the conniving liar that she is, gossiped about me to an elderly female guest at the reception desk. She flagrantly mocked me as a ***"wench with no future that everyone makes fun of."***

So, altogether, Ms. Rotten is a duplicitous, backbiting specter who slandered an innocent student for participating in spreading lies and promoted harassment towards me.

During my whole tenure at SJHS, I had Ms. Amelia as a gym teacher. For the first three and a half years, she was neutral; she didn't blatantly mock or castigate me like the other repulsive pedagogue. However, I was already aware that she must've heard the rumors since the other instructors pedaled the same lies and insults towards me.

It wasn't until Senior year in the final quarter of the semester that Ms. Amelia showed her demonic nature in gym class...by hurling insults and defaming me, like ***a mentally ill banshee***.

On the second to last gym class of my senior year, I decided to sit the period out due to mental stress of being in that tumultuous environment. Ms. Amelia was loudly calling the students' names for attendance and once she had reached my name and looked at me, I responded by shaking my head, *"No, (I'm sitting out for today)."*

At that moment, Ms. Amelia lost all semblance of humanity and transformed into **the Banshee**. It screamed in a loud voice,

"Well, she's just a whore who does nothing."

This incident occurred while all the raucous snakes were about to play dodgeball. While I stared back at her in righteous anger, after that, I wasn't surprised by her behavior.

Sometimes I noticed her conversing with Ms. Rotten, another slanderer in the main office. Since Ms. Amelia's behavior is evident of following the pervasive lies among the teachers, she also demonstrates that not all people color view each other as equals.

Adding in the ***student/teacher power dynamic***, I'm willing to pontificate, that Ms. Amelia the Banshee as well as the other faculty members mentioned here took their frustrations out on me. Not only because I was quiet, a loner, and/or my body was "too pronounced", but most importantly, they preyed on my gentle nature.

All in all, Banshee is just another worthless, sanctimonious liar, who conformed to the crowd of mental abusers and slanderers.

The last three people, mentioned here, who have either slandered or harassed me on at least one occasion, are named Mrs. Gums, another hypocritical feminist, Ms. Salome, a guidance counselor, and Mr. Ryan, an instructor I had for Sophomore biology and Senior piano class.

Starting with Ms. Gums, an art teacher and close friend to the **Corpse Hag**, I was already aware of her bias towards me when I attended her sketching class in my junior year. Unlike the other instructors, Ms. Gums wasn't outwardly hostile towards me; she always spoke to me with a smile along with the other students. But I *could not* trust her, despite her kind visage.

Attending such a vile environment after experiencing mistreatment from junior high, magnified my distaste and distrust for teachers. When it comes to Ms. Gums, she was there when the Corpse Hag was slandering me back in my sophomore year, agreeing and smiling with her. As for her beratement towards me, it was small but confirmed my suspicions.

One warm, spring day, while she was giving her lecture in the classroom, the moment she walked towards me, depressed and tired in my seat, she spoke in a muffled voice and said:

"You look disheveled," while wearing a disingenuous, *horse-like smile*, mocking my appearance, just like the other pathetic instructors.

As for Ms. Salome, ironically a counselor, also participated in backbiting against me. The incident took place during my junior year. Around April, I entered an empty classroom, waiting for the next period class to commence, after walking past two teachers who were conversing adjacent to the doorway. Ms. Salome was talking to a male instructor about the school, but after I entered, I overheard her baseless lie about me. Ms. Salome falsely stated,

"I hate her. She always uses her body to seduce the faculty," towards her male colleague.

The moment she lied, I caught her glance towards me. Considering her profession as a guidance counselor, it's the height of irony she would contribute to the mental deterioration of an innocent student, through her slander.

Finally, Mr. Ryan, while I attended his Geology class in my sophomore year, he also wasn't overtly hostile or berating me. Nevertheless, I kept my suspicions about him. The baseless rumors and lies spread among the students and faculty were the equivalent of a virus and everyone there had transformed into audacious, sadistic hivemind, who enjoyed sexually harassing me, forming more lies while gorging on the existing falsities, reveled into my depression, and humiliating me.

The incident where Mr. Ryan showcased his true nature as the **Hog;** he sexually harassed me was at the end of my sophomore year. During the Regents' Exam (state final exam), my schedule for the test rooms had an error. So, I had to wait in an empty classroom, while a teacher was preparing a revised schedule.

While I was waiting, Mr. Hog was assigned to watch me. At the time, I was extremely nervous, and worried that he would verbally abuse me.

For the next few minutes, while I was sitting at a desk in front of Mr. Hog, he was making a call on his phone. After several minutes had passed, he yelled at me in a loud voice:

"I DON'T WANT YOU!"

Predictably, he falsely accused me of trying to seduce him, even though I did nothing but sit at a desk. Afterwards, Mr. Hog continued to mumble on his phone, I remembered (in bits and pieces) he was explaining to the person on the phone that I was attempting to seduce him.

There wasn't anyone in the vicinity, and I left that room shaking in a panic once I received my new schedule. Pertaining to both mendacious, white, false accusers, as well as the disgusting pig, who's dumb as rocks, Mr. Hog, I always pondered when I was young:

Why do these supposed Christians always view me in a sexual light? Why do they assume the body of a young, black girl should be objectified?

It's no surprise Catholic instructors in general are known to abuse children, but to slander a shy, innocent girl who just wanted to be invisible, is the zenith of breaking the ninth commandment and a quick trip to the depths of hell.

Looking back on all the verbal abuse and slander these pigs put me through, and the uncontrollable shaking that was a result of it, I regret the self-hatred I had at the time.

I never wanted to be noticed by anyone, I felt nervous walking by anyone, I did not want them to notice my buxom figure. I only wanted to be by myself because I knew I could never fit in with the students and when I entered SJHS, I wanted to avoid re-experiencing the same harassment and bullying I underwent in junior high, which happened ironically. At the end of the day, I did nothing wrong, I have a clear consciousness and I have learned to love myself, body, mind, and spirit.

Now, back to the "repeat offenders" ...

"The Incident"

An event that will be referenced in the latter half of this memoir is what I dubbed ***"The Incident"***.

Early December of Senior Year, I woke up one morning, invigorated by righteous indignation and the Lord himself. I had the notion of confronting both the slutty snake students and the homeroom teacher, Mr. Judas, who also engaged in slandering and harassing me. I believed my confrontation with them would finally end the bullying and lies they inflicted on me, once and for all.

As everyone sat among their cliques and I self-ostracized as usual, I motivated my mind to face my slanderers. I walked up to Mr. Judas's desk, (who also participated in slandering/harassing me), and spouted the same insults to him, that the students and him said to me:

"Mr. Judas...I never wanted you...You faggot wuss."

"W-what?" the bespectacled coward stammered.

I turned my attention towards the snakes(students) and gave them a piece of my mind. I screamed at them for being hypocrites, sadists, and slanderers. In a scathing voice I pointed out their hypocrisy:

> ***"Who the fuck are you to call me a hoe?!***
>
> ***You nasty skanks wear your skirts up to your asses like tramps!"***

Amid my righteous indignation, my eyes started to well up with tears, I wanted this abuse, this slander this persecution to end...with my own two hands.

All the anger I held from being bullied in Jr. High and now high school was now unleashed. I continued screaming at the snakes of all the verbal abuse they inflicted on me.

I hated attending shithole SJHS, but I was afraid I would experience the same harassment if I transferred to another school, I hated everyone in that torture factory, but most of all, ***I loathe living in New York City.***

All the snakes stood silent except for a creepy predator named **Donna**, who ran to the bathroom, withholding laughter which infuriated me. I will forever call her a predator (**Pred-Donna**), because in Freshman Year, I caught her attempting to voyeuristically watch me when I was about to change my menstrual pad, in the restroom stall. Ironically, **Pred-Donna** was happily accepted among the snakes as a *"dear friend"*. What an **abhorrent, disgusting creep.**

Grace, *of all snakes,* attempted to console me, by guiding my hand (dragging) me to the restroom. Unfortunately, I let my guard down and let her hug me, slightly believing that she and maybe all the snakes could empathize with the damage their slander did to me. My inner voice, A.K.A, *"The Pit"*, informed me of Grace's façade, and…*it was right.*

A few months later, Traitor-Grace displayed her true nature and her feelings towards me. Around the end of the semester, she greeted me while I walked past her and her friends.

"Hi, [Jane]!" Grace cheerfully welcomed.

"Oh, Hello." I jadedly responded.

Not until I was five feet ahead of them, I overheard Traitor-Grace whisper and slandered me to her friends.

> ***"[Jane]'s just mad she doesn't have a boyfriend."*** She lied.

> ***"You don't know me, cuntwhore."*** I said to myself.

For a situation like this, I hated being slandered and misunderstood. Luckily, I witnessed Traitor-Grace's true nature, a sanctimonious trollop who only prioritizes social status, acts vulgar, wears a facade of loquaciousness and acceptance and values lasciviousness; A commonality between her and the snakes, which is why I call them a **mindless mob**.

Traitor-Grace only pretended to assist the loner, neurodivergent student experiencing turmoil to appear as a hero, which is the nadir of being a human. Although Grace's duplicity earned her some form of social clout, and favor among the demonic teachers, she's unaware that God favors the meek and not mendacious, toxic females like her.

At the height of my anger, during ***"the incident"*** I flipped a desk over.

Suddenly, Sleazy-C, and the ***misguidance counselor,*** Mrs. Delilah arrived at the classroom. I screamed at the pedo-corpse Sleazy-C, who was about to approach me:

"DON'T TOUCH ME!"

I did **NOT** want that harasser anywhere near me.

After I had my mental breakdown, I was taken to the ***misguidance*** counselor, Ms. Delilah, and lo and behold; faithless Sister Barabbas was there as well. In my distressed and crying state, I confessed my frustrations to Sr. Barabbas, about how the students and teachers slandered, humiliated, and harassed me up to this point and how it resulted in magnifying my anxiety, depression, and PTSD symptoms. The best solution impious Sr. Barabbas could muster,

"Try drawing a picture."

A.K.A: ***"I'm too lazy, nepotistic or wimpy to discipline students and expose the perverted teachers, who are also my friends."*** is how I interpreted it.

I was stunned at first, but that short shock transformed into realization that impious Sister Barabbas was protecting her *"friends"* in her indolent attempt to assess my trauma.

After the incompetent consultation, I was sent home early that day, on Friday. Honestly, my mother was proud of me for yelling at the sleazy snakes.

When I returned to school on Monday, Delilah, the misguidance counselor, informed me of all the slanderous classmates in homeroom arguing and panicking with each other, only fearing discipline from their negligent, worthless, single mothers. Predictably, their behavior did not cease afterwards. But the students' degeneracy is another story for another time.

"Patterns"

Ever since I was a young child, I was always hyper aware of people's idiosyncrasies, characteristics and behaviors. This trait of mine always assisted with evaluating people's character, especially which person possessed integrity or not.

I have and forever will be grateful of this talent since I noticed repetitive, malevolent, behavioral, and personality contradictions among the teachers and snakes at shithole SJHS. While the latter group has committed decadences that will be told at another time, the repeat hostility from instructors is something to be identified. For simplicity's sake, I'll call these *"patterns"*.

1) The instructors were always biased towards the lying, sadistic students.

The perpetrators of the slander towards me are a "chicken-or-the egg" situation. *Was it the snakes or the teachers who commenced it?*

However, the pedo-adjacent pedagogues were oddly biased towards the students who harassed me. They even befriended the loud and obnoxious snakes. Obviously, it's because the snakes were more sociable, expressive, and showcased a duplicitous, *"positive and quirky!"* personality.

As for me, I couldn't lie to myself, I hated attending in that degenerate, musty environment surrounded by fake, ghetto, miscreants, who screamed almost every sentence, who enjoyed backbiting me and had the nerve to call me a "friend". As honest as I was, I was not afraid to show my disgust and depression on my face. I didn't care if I came off as unapproachable, I was still courteous to those treacherous sleazebag instructors, but they had the **temerity** to curse me under their breath, in which I heard. **At the very best, I exposed** their *immature and hypocritical* nature without doing anything to them.

Even their discipline towards the student body differentiated me and the snakes. For example, in freshman year when I retaliated at an obese student by calling her a **fatass,** the ghetto snakes looked at me in (feigned) horror, and the homeroom teacher (Mr. Judas) approached me to talk. The situation was so overblown and ridiculous. Plus, the homeroom teacher **DID nothing** to stop the snakes from hollering and screeching every day, every consecutive morning.

In the middle of junior year, I was practicing how to draw a gun for an art project. When I arrived home, my mother informed me how the other students notified the *mis*guidance counselor: Mrs. Delilah, who called her, in shock and (fake) worry. ***The situation was completely idiotic, once again***.

In comparison the snakes harassed the strict, elderly English teacher, Ms. Amelie, in Junior year (Mid-April), by stomping their feet in unison as an **"April Fools' prank"** during class, thus silencing and overwhelming her.

I could tell this was done out a collective grudge due to Amelie's firmness towards them in Freshmen year. Even Zoe, one of the top, *book-smart students*, participated. Then, Ms. Amelie quickly exited out of the classroom, due to either stress, frustration, or a meltdown. Afterward, none of the snakes involved were disciplined or suspended; they just got an elongated, empty lecture from the forked-tongue principal, Sister Barabbas.

2) The teachers couldn't tolerate a neurodivergent student like me.

Considering the slanderous educators either overreacted towards my self-defense from bullying or unjustifiably, almost punishing me. It's obvious they stereotyped me as a potential *"school shooter"* for being quiet. Plus, the deviant educators ranged from elderly Boomers to Gen Xers, the generations that didn't acknowledge shyness, meekness, gentleness, and most importantly neurodivergence.

From my experience, it's obvious that sadistic pedagogue viewed a traumatized, bullied, quiet teen who had body issues and always felt stiff and awkward, like I was, as a broken doll to mistreat and abuse. Ultimately, their behavior contradicts their self-proclaimed allegiance to democratic values and Catholicism. In actuality, their natures and behaviors lean towards sociopathy and Satanism.

3) *The teachers were just as immature as the students.*

Only emotionally stunted pedos would congregate around school bullies and participate in slandering and harassing a lone student. Those filthy perverts had no concrete evidence of me attempting to seduce them, nor did they have the wherewithal of knowing my true character.

From my perspective, the slanderous faculty believed the baseless rumors perpetuated by the students and engaged along with harassing me. Furthermore, I always observed a tone of elation or unwarranted bitterness whenever these pedo-adjacent instructors defamed me discreetly or openly humiliated me in front of the whole class.

Between Freshman and Sophomore years, I always pontified, ***if these deviant teachers considered me as a problem due to my body, then why didn't they ask me?*** For example, why didn't Mrs. Corpse Hag discuss her problems with me like an adult? surely, I would've told her the truth that I or nobody else wanted her decaying, shambling walking dildo, Sleazy-C.

In reality, there was nothing wrong with me. I couldn't control how my body was shaping, and those perverted "Catholic" instructors objectified and slandered me for it. Even if they did confront me rationally, it would be discriminatory, equivalent to incidents of white instructors cutting a black student's hair, *"over school regulations"*.

Ultimately, I wouldn't be surprised if those lecherous, lying hags and potential pedos for teachers, viewed me as a punching bag for their verbal abuse, slander and sexual harassment.

4) They're sexual deviants.

If anyone saw a buxom female teen who kept to herself, *"provocative"* wouldn't be the right descriptor. So, why would these **"college-educated"** instructors assume I'm trying to seduce them?

Why would they berate me and sexually harass me due to my body?

Meanwhile, they allow the snakes to traipse in thigh-high cut skirts like prostitutes and show off their lower backs with their gelatinous muffin tops exposed.

5) Their physicality reflects their repulsiveness.

We all know the phrase: ***"What's ugly on the inside will be ugly on the outside."*** Since these chimo instructors were stupid enough to slander, berate, and sexualize me, their characters are rotten, and they possess no integrity. Was their hostility towards me based on *envying youth? Envying beauty? Or enjoying the abuse of a neurodivergent, quiet traumatized minor?*

I always disregarded the chimo pedagogues' speeches about *"positivity"* and *"unity"* because they're hollow and are malicious slanderers and perverts with no empathy. It doesn't take a fortune teller to know where these worthless corpses will go after death.

6) They hate diversity.

For a group of "*progressive*" instructors, they really enjoyed sexualizing and harassing a minority student. I do not know what's in their hearts, but objectifying and demeaning a female, minor student over her body, something she can't control is **pedophilic.**

Also, don't they understand the implications of mentally/verbally berating an innocent student? They're not disproving the "child-abusing" stereotype, indicative of Catholic schools.

By observing their actions, especially from the older white chimo teachers, it makes one wonder if they ever humanized me to begin with.

7) Toxic Femininity & Duplicity

While modern society is appraised of *toxic masculinity,* **"mean girl"** behavior, A.K.A *"toxic femininity"* is rampant and continuous due to gender biases and modern wave feminism. While toxic femininity is prevalent among the female instructors, it's pathetic to witness **even the males**, engage in this degenerate, hypocritical, effeminate and *bitchy* behavior.

If the self-proclaimed pious, Catholic school, **shithole SJHS,** practiced God's word, then it wouldn't be a hivemind of sin, slander, and hypocrisy.

"Hivemind" is the most apropos word to describe the "toxic feminine" environment that taints the halls of St. Joseph's HS. For the snakes, being loud, disruptive, ghetto, vulgar, tolerating those behaviors and associating with them will ingratiate you into the *hivemind*. As for me, I couldn't acclimate the ghetto hive of snakes due to despising loud people and that my personality was incompatible with theirs.

For the perverted faculty, being biased towards the snakes due to associating with them, believing the snakes' baseless rumors about me, and giving the snakes a *"wrist slap"* pertaining to discipline welcomed them into the *hivemind*.

When it came to me, any lie and falsity is automatically believed. The perverted instructors also engaged in sexual harassment, verbal abuse, open humiliation, adulation for slandering and harassing me and wicked sadism exactly like the snakes. It is as the saying goes: ***"Misery loves company."***

"Duplicity" is the cloak of an evil person's mask that belies the dagger he or she will stab you with. It always repulsed me how the Pedo-Pedagogue of shithole SJHS can just smile at me while slandering me under their breath with no guilt or impunity. Honestly, the sadistic pedo-pedagogues acclimate nicely with the sanctimony of the Catholic church, who claims to *"cherish the innocent"* for God, but also abuses the innocent for their perverse amusement.

"Psychological Abuse" was the norm for a loner like me in shithole SJHS. Surprisingly, the vile environment never devolved into physical abuse either between the snakes or towards me (probably due to my tall stature).

Among the sexual slander towards me, the pedo-adjacent pedagogues enjoyed yelling and humiliating me in their self-righteous form of **"correcting me"** or to satiate their fragile, vicious ego. Likewise, they also gaslighted me. While some of those nasty chimo instructors apologized to me after *"the incident,"* months later, as I expected, they continued their slander and harassment. It was impossible to expect demons like them to repent of their sinful nature.

8) Exact Type of Bullying Experienced in Jr. High

My adolescence felt like a broken record of verbal abuse, slander, and bullying. The students of St. Michael's

Academy in Flushing, Queens (Jr. High) were feral, duplicitous, perverts, deviants, sociopaths, slanderers and pretenders. The teachers were unveiled to be hostile and liars. Both groups ended up spreading lies, hurling sexual remarks at me, and even worse ruining my reputation throughout the whole neighborhood.

Between St. Michael's and St. Joseph's, both school principals **were sisters**. ***Mrs. Willy*** and ***Sister Barabbas*** really had a knack for creating hellholes from religious facilities.

9) *Was the school meant to be for delinquents?*

Shithole SJHS possess definite trademarks of a delinquent school: unruly, double-crossing, undisciplined students, perverted abusive teachers and hilariously **lack of essential equipment** and **allowing random adults to enter.**

Throughout all four years of me attending that dung-hole of a school. There was never a **Nurse's station/office**. *Nor was there any intention of creating one.* If a student were to be injured either in gym class (physical) or in chemistry class, the only treatment she would receive is either an ice pack or a quick shower and a visit to the office with a prayer for a quick ambulance. ***Hypothetically,*** if that pregnant classmate in the same grade as I, had a complication (actuality, she had a safe delivery) would Sister Barabbas and Sleazy-C take responsibility?

Don't they realize time is the utmost essence in the event of serious injuries? Seemingly, the physicality of maturing female adolescents is handwaved for money.

I'm fully convinced that ***Mammon, the Archdemon of Greed,*** is the real patron saint of Shithole SJHS. What else is the main reason for renting out the school to random adults? For all four years of my tenure, half of the third floor was under construction for a lawyer's office. When the *misguidance counselor* informed the class of what it'll be, my first thought was:

"What kind of idiot lawyer would commence their practice in a building where the bell rings every forty minutes?"

Hilarity aside, what if the lawyer's clients are/were potential criminals that haven't been incarcerated yet? Yet the school intended to place that kind of business alongside "vulnerable" students.

Furthermore, floors 8-10 were relegated to GED students. Even though SJHS students and they were ***efficiently separated***, I remember the most of GEDs were a majority of non-white men (*probably foreigners*) and very few women, who both barely fluent in English, whenever they rode the elevator from the first floor. This is comparable to a pack of wolves separated from a hen farm through a thin, wooden fence; a terrible situation is bound to occur from this.

More disturbingly, none of the students' parents/guardians were ever notified about this via letter or email. It's obvious that if parents knew, there would be a lot more transfers.

Logically, my solution would be to schedule GED classes in the evenings and weekends for floors 8-10. As essential, install a nurse's office on the third floor which is between the auditorium (gym class) and the chemistry room (5th floor) so injured students won't have to travel far.

Finally, have the lawyer's office on the 9th or 10th floor, so no minors will be in proximity. Better yet, **shithole SJHS** should've hold more school events like bake sales, charities, and talent shows for donations, so the faculty wouldn't have to **whore out** the century-old school building. More importantly, why didn't the Diocese help the school, if Catholicism was founded on generosity?

But hey, *it really says something* when a depressed, introverted, asocial, neurodivergent, traumatized writer has more business sense than a school official.

Unsurprisingly, the snakes tended to subtly break the uniform code. By subtly, I mean the secrecy of a skunk's odor range. The snakes followed a disgusting trend of pulling their blouses up to display their lower backs. **If it were legal**, the snakes that engaged in that trend would have *definitely*, gotten *"tramp stamp"* tattoos. Speaking of which, a snake by the name of Amy, donned an arm tattoo, and guess what? No school discipline, *as usual!*

Likewise, the carnality of displaying the lower back varied among the different grades and revoltingly… differing *body types*.

Practically every day, **my eyes were assaulted** with the horrible visage of gut-spilling, overweight and the occasional obese snakes grandstanding their muffin tops with deep, multiple ***watermelon stripe* stretchmarks,** accentuated with a musty odor, that wafted in the air, when multiple corpulent snakes crowded the hallway. They were all deluded to be as attractive as *"Sports Illustrated"* models. It was wretch-inducing. I couldn't fathom the snakes' mirage of assuming that **ANY** of them could attract a mate.

As for the skinnier snakes, they tended to get away with hiking their skirts up above their knees or mid-thighs. Surprisingly, the fatter snakes knew they would stick out like an *elephant in the room* if they emulated the same behavior. Finally, the third group of snakes that did neither of those trends openly befriended the snakes that broke uniform code, which leaves their integrity and morals to be questioned, especially when these snakes openly berated me. Once again, the **lazy pedagogues of shithole SJHS never disciplined** the snakes for turning their uniforms into *"whore rags"*.

Hypocritically, I remember (junior year) the chemist teacher, Mrs./Ms. Vain waiting for the elevator, and just like the snakes, had her lower back exposed, in a worthless

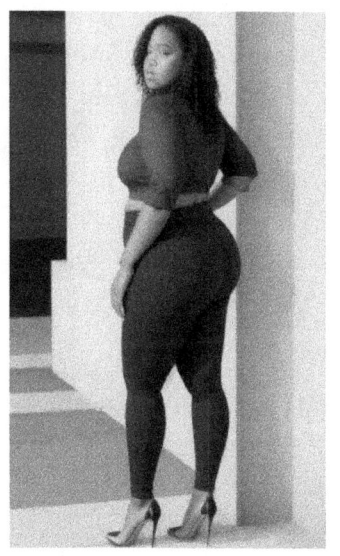

attempt to feel young. ***How pathetic.*** Since underaged degeneracy was the norm in the shithole school, it's evident, that the snakes were products of *"early sexualization of girls"* that raided modern culture as well as black and brown communities. However, I refuse to see the snakes as victims, since ***they chose*** to modify their uniforms, act vulgar, and chose to slander me as "promiscuous" for my body, while being cognizant to earn college scholarships. Well for me, ***I chose*** to expose the depravity of *Sodom & Gomorrah* disguised as a Catholic school.

(*Left: A.I. representation of shithole SJHS snakes wearing their uniforms, with no heels.*)

Tiredly, Halloween wasn't spared from any decency. The snakes were so brazening in their costumes that resemble jezebels ensnaring "Johns". I remember witnessing and being astonished in Freshman year, at two snakes who dressed up in Brittany Spears' slutty schoolgirl outfit from her "*Hit Me Baby One More Time,*" music video (***Minnie***) and the other snake dressed up as a *"Don Magic Juan"*-like pimp (***Avery***). As usual, those costumes weren't rebuked. In all honestly, it's surprising that shithole SJHS, wasn't destroyed by fire like the two most unholy cities in the Bible.

Conclusively, Sister Barabbas and Sleazy-C turned shithole SJHS into a "***metaphorical brothel***" for Lord knows how long. Between the snakes dressing like trollops, being loud, harassing students, and the repulsive pedagogues renting this place to anyone and anywhere in this school showcases, that access to students, ***comes with a certain price.***

10) Generational Divide or...Hatred?

Referring to ***"Pattern #2"***, I've observed since the start of my adolescence, that **Baby Boomers, Gen Xers,** and **older generations**, *outside of my family* tend to be irrationally hostile, or begrudgingly malicious towards me. That unneeded anger I received from them was evident during Jr. High, around my neighborhood, during my college years, and **shithole SJHS was no better.**

Considering the faculty was flippant on ***"the incident"***, as well as their continual slander and harassment from both them and the snakes, they devalued me, just because I was a neurodivergent, quiet, depressed loner, with no social status, and was misjudged for my body. It's pathetic that these so-called *"educators"* confuse shyness and meekness for weakness, a buxom physique for promiscuity and obviously, their arrogance in claiming to know everything about just from baseless rumors.

Hypothetically, if I were to confront the repulsive pedagogue from shithole SJHS, they would most likely respond with the most ***Boomer-tier*** excuses to justify their defamation:

- *"It happened so long ago!"*
Historical events happened a long time ago. Let go of them.

- *"Don't be so negative!"*
Don't avoid the truth about your slander and harassment, you coward.

- *"They're just words!"*
So are *Huckleberry Finn* and *Mein Kampf*. But you skeletons can't handle nuance, context, history, or those books without censoring them.

- *"I didn't mean to! I'm so sorry!"*
You're only sorry because you've been exposed.

- *"I don't remember."*
How do you know you're innocent then?

- *"It made you tougher, didn't it?"*
How do PTSD, insomnia, defamation and stressful flashbacks, make you tough?

- *"You let it happen."*
You started this defamation and were the cause of this memoir to be published.

- "I didn't know you were being slandered."

You hung around teachers/snakes who also slandered me. I also noticed you rarely disciplined them too.

11) ***Some things to learn from them.***
Well, those worthless chimos taught me not to befriend women or "men" who gossip and spread rumors like females.

As an addendum, I've discovered another student's written anecdote that coincides with mine, describing the vile pedagogues. According to her account, the unstable, (and only) unprofessional piano instructor for the seniors was, **Mr. Ryan the Hog** (who I also had to learn from). Not only was he lackadaisical, but he rarely showed any effort into disciplining the snakes. Predictably, Sister Barabbas' greed for money and ineptitude over school policies/student safety was emphasized. At the very least, I'm somewhat elated that former alumni have noticed the true, disgusting, depraved nature of the pedo-pedagogy that comprised of Shithole SJHS.

Dec 11, 2014

① First to Review

I didn't like the school system and the way the principal run the school. Examples:1. The teachers: Most of the teachers are nice but some are very rude. i can tell you i always been a good student i always do my work and i don't answer back. Some of the teacher don't teach, For example i had a piano class with a certain teacher and he would just sit and eat and not teach us and was very rude to me when i ask for new batteries he suck his teeth and grab the piano from my hand . Then at the end of the year we had to practice and perform a song. but i couldn't cause i didn't have batteries for two weeks. I told my mom about it and she had to come to school and talk to him on the phone. After he kept yelling and me and treating me bad when it was not my fault. His suppose to provide batteries.2. The principle: i felt like the Principle puts up an act when she with parents and she is friendly to them and make them think the school is a good school. i didn't like the way she treat the students. I believe all she care about is money and collecting fundraiser money every year and i never saw any improvements expect Smartboards. 3. The Students: They have good students their but they had a lot of bad kids there and badly influencing people. when i was still in school their were a lot of bullying and fighting going on in the school. And the principle did nothing about it a lot of girls who should of gotten expelled didn't. And it was the same group of girls a lot them mostly cared about looks and how people dress and how people look. i didn't like the way the principle handled the situation like giving the whole class lecture like we all did something wrong. other example is when we went on a class retreat and it was mandatory. One girl decide to bring weed and smoke with three other girls and one got expelled and other three got to stay and two of them got to go to Prom. Other example is when girl in my class was bringing alcohol to school drinking in class. When the principle found out she prevent my class from drinking water or any liquid in a bottle if it was not in the cafeteria. if you wanted water you would have to get it directly from the water fountain that sometimes taste very weird. If the principle or other teacher see you drink they apparently had the right to take away from you or tell you to put it away. Just because they was scared that in a water bottle or any other bottle there was alcohol in it.

Chapter Four

<u>Sister Barabbas (Principal) and Mrs. Delilah (Guidance Counselor)</u>

If there were any more evidence that I could elucidate how my slanderers ranged from the loud, ghetto freshman students to the head of this shithole school, look no further than the priggish, with an eloquent, yet *silver-forked* tongue, the principal, **Sister Barabbas**. Also, a rotting, walking contradiction to her profession, the hypocritical, bad-mouthing guidance counselor, Mrs. Delilah (*who is undeserving of her full name, relating to prominent Biblical figures*).

Her mistreatment towards me fits the title of **"Misguidance Counselor"** and the fact that she contributed to the mental suffering of a black student, Resulting in dramatic irony. Her slander, which consisted of the same insults from other teachers, was a gradual process throughout my four-year tenure at Shithole SJHS.

Starting from Freshman year, the haggard, bag of bones, Delilah, would either look disgusted as I walked by her or mutter:

> ***"No one wants to see that,"*** referring to my prominent hips.

What's even more disingenuous, she had the gall to act pleasantly to my face in all our interactions, to hide her irrational hostility to me. After realizing Delilah's duplicitous nature early on, she became another, disgusting liar who would falsely judge me as promiscuous due to my early maturation. Ironically, she did a stupendous job in not building trust among me, a student. Predictably, the students who opened to her were the same ones who would harass and slander me. Thus, proving my point that this duplicitous, sham of a school was mired in lies and hypocrisy.

Continuing Delilah's unwanted distaste for me, in mid-spring of Sophomore year, at the beginning of her guidance class. Once I approached my seat, I noticed her conversing with a relative. The part of the conversation I overheard was her slandering me by inferring I was "easy," "promiscuous" and unwanted. She mentioned,

> ***"Well, [Jane] will never have a ring on her finger."***

Thus, continuing her spurious, slanderous nature.

At the end of my sophomore year, after completing the final subject Regent's exam, I said my goodbyes to her, who was the proctor. Once, I closed the door, I overheard Delilah say,

> ***"She'll end up being a prostitute,"*** slandering me over my body once again.

Peculiarly, in the middle of Junior Year, ***"Misguidance Counselor"*** Delilah revealed to the class about her sexual assault. While I empathized with her plight, her hostile behavior towards me was irrational, repetitive, and unnecessary. ***Why did she berate me for my body*** when **she should know** it's not a female's fault for being assaulted? In my case, being harassed/slandered. Judging from her continual slander of me, one would confuse Delilah as the type of ignoramus to blame a female for what she was wearing after an assault.

Maybe I'm too logical to comprehend the hypocrisy of a duplicitous, unctuous liar. Was the ***"Misguidance Counselor"*** projecting her tragedy? Was she projecting her blame onto me? Who knows. At the end of the day, liars like her will enter the gates of hell regardless of their circumstances.

A memorable event of her never-ending hypocrisy was ***"the incident".*** I had a traumatic breakdown due to all the verbal abuse, stress, slander, and harassment that both the student body and the faculty had inflicted on me.

In Delilah's office, I explained all the abuse I underwent to her and the principal, Sister Barabbas. In hindsight, I hated that I still trusted that worthless authority that was also the cause of ruining my reputation and my mental distress.

Subsequently, after they gave me the worst advice on how to contend with harassment. The moment I was about to leave the office, sanctimonious Delilah said,

> ***"Ugh, no one wants to see that,*** *"*denigrating my character over my body once again.

Evidently, a liar like her can never tell the truth, even if you were to rip out her tongue.

When the principal of a "religious" school engages in the denigration of a student, it is evident the whole establishment is corrupt. After all, a sexual harassment scandal at a Catholic school is horribly predictable in modern society.

While I have overheard Sister Barabbas belittled me three times, those situations were enough to determine how hypocritical, traitorous, and incompetent she truly was. Furthermore, if anyone was foolish enough to befriend Sleazy-C and the Corpse Hag, *as well as* allow them to work around minors, then his/her character and integrity is demonstrably atrocious.

The first incident occurred in the early months of Sophomore year. It started a day after I heard ***Grace***, bragging about ***wanting to shove her used menstrual pad/tampon in my face*** to her two friends. In my already depressed, traumatized state, with no one in school to rely on, I relayed the incident to my mother, who called and lambasted Sister Barabbas to punish/discipline Grace before the bullying from the students elevated to any level of severity.

The next morning, during homeroom, Sister Barabbas visited the classroom and discussed the matter with Grace and the teacher, Mr. Judas, adjacent to the doorway. While I walked past the trio, the faithless Sister Barabbas said to Grace:

"Don't worry...She'll [Jane] just run to her mother," castigating me for Grace's vile, potential, threat and protecting her.

Internally, I wanted to invade the treacherous trio and scream at Barabbas for her deformation of me.

Sister Barabbas's second incident of belittlement towards me was in Senior Year, on the day of *"the incident"*, early December, her lackadaisical approach to my sexual harassment.

Another event that solidified Sister Barabbas's deformation of me, occurred near the end of Senior Year. On a hot, summer day, I signed my name at the front desk, to relax in the library, which was customary for the students.

As I did, Sister Barabbas guiding a young, black, female, would-be Freshman around the school. She was uncomfortably close with the minor, putting her arm around her shoulder, overfamiliarly. The two of them were conversing at the trophy case, adjacent to the library entrance. I overheard Sister Barabbas lying to the would-be Freshman:

"Stay away from her [Jane]. She's the school whore."

Like Saint Peter denying his discipleship with Jesus three times, this repulsive, mendacious, worthless excuse of a principal slandered and defamed my character with her deceitful tongue. Keep in mind, Sister Barabbas conversed and dismissed any other female students who paraded the halls with their skirts hiked up to their thighs, allowed them to expose their lower backs, (*surprisingly, there weren't any tramp stamps, but watermelon stripes around their FUPAs, hilariously*) and permitted the snakes to don whorish costumes every Halloween.

My parents always joked about Sister Barabbas being a closet lesbian, just from her appearance and mannerisms. Reminiscing on her permissiveness towards the snakes' degeneracy via showing off skin and her overfamiliarity towards them raises the question of whether only Sr. Barrabas prioritized money (to keep the unruly students attending) or possessed a *lustful gaze* towards the snakes. Her actions speak louder than her words. But I'll let you make the inference, *dear reader*.

Hypocritically, when one student in the same grade as me, got pregnant during Sophomore year, Sister Barabbas nor the other teachers didn't separate or disparage her (***probably because of her social circle of raucous trollops***).

Baseless rumors about me aside, I'm willing to bet Sister Barabbas and the other predatory teachers viewed the depressed, quiet, loner student like me as weak and worthless, contradicting the Catholic Christian notion of ***"[wearing] tender mercies, kindness and humility..."* (Colossians 3:12 KJV),** breaking the ninth commandment, and disgracing the honorable name of Joseph, Jesus' earthly father that mentored him about the world, via their mistreatment of me, a student, and their allowance of the student body's depravity.

As I have stated before, sexual perversion and Catholicism are synonymous. If I could change the past, I wish that I avoided the Catholic pedagogical institutions I attended for junior and high school. But alas, exposing the evil and maltreatment I experienced is the best retribution and the ultimate, objective truth I can unveil to the world.

Additionally, to Sister Barabbas's devilish nature. I would like to include another aspect of her corrupt behavior, ***greed***. Not only does her forked tongue spout lies, platitudes and empty promises, but it also craves and desires money, ***loving the root of all evil (1 Timothy 6:10 KJV).***

At the end of Senior Year, I decided to opt out of prom (horribly decorated) and the graduation ceremony due to my declining mental health, the constant burnout I had from the stressful environment and as a ***one-person protest.***

I only wanted to obtain my diploma, plus the seniors had to pay out of their own pockets (*around $200*) for their cap and gown. Furthermore, my family and I were economically destitute at the time which gave me more credence to avoid the ceremony and obviously, out my disgust for shithole SJHS.

With the price of tuition, plus the financial aid from scholarships, it made me wonder why Sister Barabbas *was lacking the funds to purchase the caps and gowns herself.* But hey, God only knows what she did with the money. It's just my speculation.

On the day of graduation practice, Sister Barabbas was appalled (blatantly feigning concern) that I didn't attend, then called my late mother in faux outrage and compassion.

Predictably, I had a habit of avoiding major school events at shithole SJHS, but *now* was the time Sister Barabbas pretended to be concerned. ***Seriously, was she in dire straits to siphon $200 from me?*** To summarize, the phone exchange between Sister Barabbas and my mother went along like this:

Mom: "[Jane] isn't attending the graduation ceremony, and she won't be paying for the cap or gown either."

Sister Barabbas: "Why?"

Mom: "The other students kept slandering and harassing her."

Sister Barabbas: "What AM I SUPPOSSED TO DO?!"

Sister Barabbas: "Look, I want to talk to [Jane] after I hand her the diploma.

This whole exchange was fucking retarded.

A few days later, when the semester and graduation were finally over. I begrudgingly hauled myself to SJHS in the late June summer heat. After I got my diploma from the barely empty head office, I **had** to attend the principal's office and then be subjected to Sister Barabbas' banal lecture and empty, worthless, platitudes.

While maintaining eye contact with her, I tuned out my attention and awareness because, ***why would I listen to a slanderous, incompetent, greedy cuntrag, who enabled my harassment and defamed my character?***

For some odd reason, Sleazy-C was in the office too, but weirdly reticent throughout Sister Barabbas's pointless speech.

Once she was done, we said our goodbyes, and I was relieved to *finally* leave that shithole school. The scars of being verbally abused, sexually harassed, being castigated and disrespected by lying, hypocritical, trollop students and predatory teachers still run deep and exacerbated the same anxiety and depression I suffered from being bullied in Jr. High. Considering Sister Barabbas's greed and incompetence, it's no wonder ***shithole SJHS finally shut down in 2019.***

Chapter Five

Mr. Judas (9-10th grade History teacher & 9-12th grade Homeroom), Mr. Measly (11th-12 grade Computer teacher) and Mr. David (12th grade English teacher)

What does it say when a new person enters a work environment and chooses to engage in defamation, hypocrisy, degeneracy and mendacity, just to be **ingratiated into a group of debauches?**

I view it as *pathetic sycophancy.* These three degenerates are no different. Just like the other chimo-pedagogues at **shithole SJHS,** Judas, Measly and David acclimated to the noxious, abusive environment and found it suitable to defame and sexually harass me. Over the course of my tenure, I managed to observe their magnanimous façade decay like rotten fruit, exposing their putrid core of soullessness. Honestly, to notice their gradual behavior shift from cordial to demeaning, from new, arriving teachers demonstrates that:

- I can rouse the worse traits out of anyone without doing anything to them.
- They were ingratiated into the *"mob mentality"* of slandering and harassing me.
- They eventually displayed their ***true, repulsive nature to me, with no remorse.***
- Despite being college educated, they really can't think for themselves or comprehend logically.

Therefore, I have decided to name this trio: *"Sons of Sleazy-C."* This moniker is appropriate for them for sharing commonalities with the **vice-principal pervert, Sleazy-C,** Mr. Cain.

Mr. Judas was affable and gregarious as well as a self-proclaimed former journalist and lawyer (in his words). Admittedly, he was excellent at teaching history. While the first few weeks of Freshman year were satisfactory in his history class, I noticed some of the snakes were spreading rumors about me attempting to seduce Mr. Judas. It was highly imbecilic, as I thought.

Even though I recognized the similar pattern of bullying from my experience in jr. high, my adolescent self, slightly, naively believed that maybe ***at least one teacher and/or a student*** wouldn't believe the rumors about me. I slightly hoped that someone wouldn't judge me based on my appearance.

Oh, how wrong I was.

One day, in mid-autumn of Freshman year, some weeks after Sleazy-C's fledgling harassment and the snakes' rumormongering. The snakes and I were entering the classroom for the afternoon history class. Judas was near the first row of desks and as I walked by him to reach for a seat:

"I don't want you." He mumbled.

The moment I heard that, my first thought was: ***"He's one of them now."***

At the time, the snakes were already pushing Idiot Judas to his limits by screaming every morning, hiking up their skirts and spouting loud vulgarities. ***How the hell did that imbecile believe their lies and start falsely accusing the quiet, loner student who kept to herself?***

Maybe, Idiot Judas took his impotent, unjustifiable slander out on me to avoid the wrath of the ghetto snakes' parents.

Furthermore, I wouldn't be surprised if Idiot Judas followed Sleazy-C's defamations about me, either. Whether or not either group convinced him first, Judas was still a troglodyte for believing the lies of sexual degenerates and hypocrites like the snakes and Sleazy-C.

By next year, Idiot Judas had gotten a bit brazen, but still stupid. He only slandered me once and in Sophomore year, he struck again.

After the class of snakes and I arrived at homeroom on the first day of school/orientation day, everyone dispersed and focused on their miniscule cliques.

However, as a loner, *I was apt to observing everyone* and got to hear tidbits of bragging about their tedious summer vacations. I didn't intend to eavesdrop, most of the snakes were inept at having an *"inside voice"*. Idiot Judas was no exception, as I was able to overhear his shallow judgement of me from his desk, as he talked to himself.

"[Jane's] about as attractive as a platypus."

Part of me wanted to run up to his desk and scream and hurl insults at him for ridiculing my appearance and falsely accusing me of seducing him.

Before everyone entered the classroom, I only had a short discussion about summer vacation with him as we and the rest of the snakes walked up the stairs. After overhearing this, I wondered at the time:

"Did that dumbass assume I was trying to hit on him during our conversation?"

Considering I already had anxiety and was hyper-vigilant over people harassing me over my appearance. That moment made me realize I have another *"enemy"* who joined the ***"slander mob mentality"*** in shithole SJHS.

From Junior to Senior years, Idiot Judas became gradually, brazenly duplicitous and disrespectful. Dare I say, twofaced as Sleazy-C.

In Junior year, approximately spring, in homeroom, a few snakes were crowding around Idiot Judas's desk over an academical problem one morning. I remember the snakes in that crowd were: Amy, Zoe, Vivi, Traitor-Grace and Pred-Donna. The bell for the first class was about to ring, so I quickly walked through the crowd of snakes, who clicked their tongues in frustration. Then, Amy, in her most **annoying, squeaky,** *"Dijonay from the Proud Family"*, clone voice uttered:

"You know he [Idiot Judas] be lookin'!"

"That's not my fault, dumbass." I said to myself.

In reference to that event, it highlighted Idiot Judas's bias and lack of discipline toward the snakes and their slander of me. Also, he deserves the title(s) of idiot, ignoramus, dumbass, pervert, scumbag and troglodyte.

*How did Idiot Judas conclude that the loner, quiet, neurodivergent student is trying to romance him(**yuck**), while believing the **skanky snakes** that trod around in their exposed backs, muffin tops and hiked up skirts like whores?*

It's evident as to why Idiot Judas couldn't make it as a "**journalist**" or "**lawyer**". He was far too stupid to *"see both sides of the story"* and too biased to capture a fair opinion.

I'm willing to bet he was equally immature as the snakes since that worthless piece of shit saw it was fair to denigrate an unpopular, loner student with PTSD from bullying.

Continuing his moral decay, *(as if he had any morals to begin with),* I caught Idiot Judas snickering with a couple of snakes in homeroom, one morning. The event occurred either in junior or senior year. The moment I walked past the putrid trio, Idiot Judas opened his dung hole of a mouth and gossiped to the snakes:

"She's [Jane] going to be made fun of in college."

Once again, that filthy, worthless pervert of an instructor continued to harass a neurodivergent student while he associated and acted like trash. It's hilarious when reprobates have no self-reflection.

As for senior year, I was fully aware of Idiot Judas's fake compassion. One commonality between **ALL** the pedo-adjacent pedagogues, *especially the men* at **shithole**

SJHS was their true, rotten natures reached an apex, shortly after I turned eighteen.

A week or two after ***"the incident"***, Idiot Judas gave me a hug and an empty speech about helping me. I could tell it was all performative, just like Traitor-Grace's false compassion: of "playing the hero". From my perspective, Idiot Judas had already metamorphized into a duplicitous turd with no soul, from all the times he berated me and trusted the lies of the snakes.

On an early spring morning in homeroom class, senior year, I was reading a book, while the snakes were loud and chatty as usual. I decided to look around the room and then noticed the snakes were surrounding Idiot Judas, who was stapling pictures of the Senior retreat and college acceptance letters onto a bulletin board.

Succinctly, the Senior retreat was a three-day trip to an upstate New York camp for *"spiritual enlightenment"*. It took place in the same week as Thanksgiving. I decided to opt-out for obvious reasons, plus, the snakes were still malicious even after the *"spiritual enlightenment"*.

I slightly watched the shitpile group (snakes & Idiot Judas) "ooooh-ing" and "aaaah-ing" over the retreat pictures and acceptance letters. In the middle of doing so, I heard Idiot Judas mention colleges and then muttered to the snakes:

"She's [Jane] only good for blowjobs," sexually harassing and slandering me, especially for something miniscule as not choosing a college/not being accepted by one, yet, at the time.

After Idiot Judas made that putrid remark with a sadistic smirk, I gave him and the snakes an indignant glare, in response to his degeneracy and immaturity.

Character-wise, Idiot Judas is similar to Sleazy-C, in being twofaced, slanderous and a sexual deviant, under a false kindly, mask.

The only difference between him and the geriatric pervert is that Idiot Judas was a ***cowardly bitch*** to harass me to my face, and too obsequious by following the crowd of snakes and pedo-adjacent pedagogues' lies about a singular, lone, depressed student, with a curvy body and who just wanted to be left alone yet respected as a human being.

For a self-proclaimed Catholic such as him, Idiot Judas should be well aware about these verses:

"He that hideth hatred with lying lips, and he that uttereth a slander, is a fool." (Proverbs 10:18 KJV).

"A false witness that speaketh lies, and he that soweth discord among brethren." (Proverbs 6:19 KJV).

Then, look in the mirror, and swallow a shotgun.

It was Orientation Day (first day of class) in Junior year, when Mr. Measly was introduced to the school by Sister Barabbas. I sat in the audience among the snakes, filled with dread and depression. Part of me expected he would be designated for the younger students, but most importantly, internally, I predicted:

"He'll join the mob mentality and ridicule me. Just like the rest of the trashy teachers and filthy snakes."

Unfortunately, Measly was the **only** teacher for computer class, and I had to contend with him for both Junior and Senior years. As usual, his behavior towards me shifted as time went on, from mild-mannered (like Idiot Judas) to a slanderous, disgusting deviant, falsely accusing me of trying to seduce him, due to baseless rumors and judging me based on my curvy physique. Even though I've done nothing to him, I had to deal with the brunt of his sexual harassment and verbal abuse.

For the first few weeks, Measly was cordial in class, but starting in early autumn, junior year. He commenced showing his deviant behavior.

Whenever the snakes and I enter the computer room, he would normally greet them, from the desk adjacent to the doors, with *"Hellos!"*. However, after I entered the room, he muttered a worthless phrase:

"I don't want that."

Just like the other pedo-pedagogues, Mr. Measly judged me based on my physique and made false assumptions of me. From then on, Measly would utter that phrase like a **demented parrot** whenever I entered the computer room but ignored the snakes' vulgarities and obviously followed the baseless rumors.

When Senior year commenced, the first couple of months were somewhat peaceful. However, I could tell the harassment would continue from the snakes, the pedo-pedagogues and clearly Mr. Measly.

Starting from autumn, whenever the wicked gnome would check everyone's work in Photoshop class (*highly useless*) by walking to each student's seat, he would mutter a lascivious, repulsive phrase in my vicinity. After he checked my work and focused on the snake next to me, he muttered:

"She doesn't even have any tits."

As much as I wanted to punch that sleazy goblin, for sexually harassing me and falsely accusing me of seducing him. I did the only thing I could do, which was to ignore him. While, doing so, that pansy troll's remark always filled me with a deadly cocktail of anxiety and righteous indignation.

After all, all the pedo-pedagogues, the incompetent principal and vice-head of **shithole SJHS were all against me.** In terms of character, Mr. Measly was a ***complete vacuous bootlicker*** to the lies uttered by the mass of snakes and chimo-teachers. I say this because at the time, the malicious gnome copied the same insult the snakes were hurling at me as well. Furthermore, Mr. Measly's teaching credits and degrees are utterly worthless if he lacks the brain capacity to not mistreat any loner students.

Throughout the months, the imbecilic parrot, Mr. Measly, continued that same sexual insult towards my body until the end of senior year. Precisely, at the second to last computer class, Mr. Measly hurled that same phrase except, more audibly, after inspecting the work on my computer.

While that event triggered another anxiety attack, I attempted to stay calm at his disgusting remark and vile demeanor. Weirdly, none of the snakes laughed in unison, they just stayed silent, which I took as an affirmation to his sexual harassment.

At the end of it all, the meager coward, Mr. Measly didn't even **man up** to say it to my face. Hell, he wasn't even mature or smart enough to confirm or ignore the rumors about me. Mr. Measly is just an insignificant worm, who most likely ingratiated and enjoyed harassing me to compensate for his low worth, lack of morals and lack of intelligence and physicality.

Comparing Mr. Measly to Sleazy-C, they both share the duplicity as well as cowardice in facing me. Ultimately, Mr. Measly, well earned his title: ***"Son of Sleazy-C"***.

Despite his scrawny physique and mild-mannered demeanor, I could tell there was something shady about Mr. David. On Orientation Day, Freshman Year, was the day I witnessed his true self.

During the first day of school, Sister Barabbas organized a juvenile game for the newly Freshman to collect stamps from various faculty and add them to their stamp board. It was a gamifying way to acquaint the students with the faculty. Even as a teenager, I found this to ***be annoying and childish***.

Back then, I was highly self-conscious about my buxom body, specifically my noticeable hips, and regretfully I used to partially blame myself, when someone falsely accused me of trying to seduce them.

While playing this stupid stamp game, my mind kept racing to one statement:

> ***"I hope no one berates me or demean me for my appearance."***

Unfortunately, I had to collect a stamp from a male instructor, which made me doubly uncomfortable. Nevertheless, I steeled myself and approached Mr. David. After collecting a stamp, I turned around and heard:

"I don't want to see that." David mumbled.

That moment, plus the snide comments from the older grade snakes at Freshmen Orientation signified the future interactions and environment that I would experience at **shithole SJHS**.

"I'm going to be slandered here, aren't I? This place is no different from St. Michaels." I realized.

I didn't have Mr. David as a teacher until Senior year, English class. Already aware of my situation of being slandered, I wasn't surprised when I discovered he was also apart the *"slander mob mentality"* at shithole SJHS.

The first incident occurred in autumn, English class. Beforehand, I was cursed to sit in the front row due to the seats assigned by the students' last names, which amplified my anxiety and negativity. Sitting in the front row ignited my fear of being harassed, slandered, and humiliated by the instructor.

On that certain day, the class was discussing *Hamlet*. As David was right above me, lecturing the snakes, I had another anxiety attack. My heart was beating rapidly, my legs were starting to shake, and I attempted to calm myself with short breaths. I loathed being anxious, for I believed it was a sign of weakness. In a quick moment, ***Mr. PDF-File*** (David) slandered me in front of the whole class. He muttered:

> ***"I don't want your vagina,"*** like the disgusting pervert he is, exactly like Mrs. Ramses.

His revolting comment was heard by the snakes in the first two columns of seats, on which a few of them laughed and agreed with Mr. PDF-File. I felt so angry and humiliated, but I had to keep myself calm, to sate my anxiety reaction and rapidly pounding, heart.

Early spring is where the second incident occurred. Between March and April, after I turned eighteen, the snakes and I were taking a test one afternoon. The classroom was shockingly quiet to hear a mouse squeak. While I focused on the test, I heard disturbing, perverted comments from Mr. PDF-File, while he was sitting at his desk.

"[Jane] looks do-able."

"Yeah, I wouldn't mind sleeping with her."

Mr. PDF-File gleefully muttered under his sick breath and vomitous smile.

Hearing those gross statements, I wanted to treat Mr. PDF-File like a punching bag. I loathed him and everyone else at **shithole SJHS.** I pontified:

"Where did these filthy, predatorial pedagogues get the nerve to sexualize their students?"

I quickly finished the English exam, handed it in, and walked away in disgust, horror and revulsion.

Mr. PDF-File's last sexual harassment occurred on the last day of regular class. All the snakes dispersed into groups and discuss as well as dissect a piece of literature. I decided to pair up with two snakes to get this class project over and done with it. While my group was ready to speak, and Mr. PDF-File was pacing around the others and hearing their dissertations, I volunteered to speak for my group, which was very bold for a quiet person such as I.

However, my voice was raspy at the time, (which I hated when that happened) and I had to clear my throat a few times. I wanted to sound clear and concise, so I could be taken seriously. When it was my group's turn to be visited, I explained and deconstructed the literature to an excellent degree, to Mr. PDF-File, that even he was amazed.

I was elated that my group finished the assignment. However, Mr. PDF-File emulated a *cowardly, mostly toxic feminine, tactic* from Mr. Measly. After he was finished with my group, Mr. PDF-File headed towards the next one and loudly hurled a sexual slur in my vicinity, too gutless to confront me and falsely accusing me again:

"Quit talking in a high pitch voice, slut."

"I know you're trying to tempt me with that voice."

The other snakes didn't react to Mr. PDF-File's pathetic tantrum. But I took their silence as affirmation. As for me, I was a bit frazzled because I didn't expect it, and once again it reawakened another short anxiety attack. But that anxiety quickly morphed into disgust and righteous anger. As the group project quickly ended, Mr. PDF-File hugged each snake, as they left the classroom. I was so disgusted at that twofaced sleazebag for trying to be friendly after brazenly slandering me.

For retaliation, I looked him dead in the eye with a "revolting" glare as though he was a walking piece of shit. I displayed that notion through my body language that I didn't want to be hugged by a filthy pervert like him. Mr. PDF-File took the hint, and I walked past him. That worthless scumbag said nothing.

Character-wise, Mr. PDF-File shares the borderline preying/lusting of students just like Sleazy-C towards that white-Hispanic female student. Furthermore, they both share a performative façade of kindness that belies an abyss of depravity. Finally, just like the other two *"Sons of Sleazy-C",* they blamed me and my body, for their perversions because they're too weak and sadistic to control their carnalities.

Honestly, it's no surprise **shithole SJHS**, hired duplicitous, terrible instructors like the *"Sons of Sleazy-C".* The school exudes degeneracy, hypocrisy, and malevolence, just like the people it invites, teachers and students alike. Part of me wonders, that maybe *some* or *most* of the instructors tolerated working at **shithole SJHS** was to engage in degenerate behavior with no repercussions. I can't imagine the pay would suffice since

SJHS was being whored out and most of the equipment was a decade old. Also, since the pedo-pedagogues enjoyed slandering/humiliating me along with the snakes, I bet they stayed there just to hang around and be immature along with them.

After all, how do you explain evil teachers befriending slanderous, sleazy, students?

Chapter Six

<u>Mrs. Samantha (9th grade Biology & 12th grade Intro Psychology teacher), Mrs. Bonny (Spanish 1&3 teacher)</u>

Last, and certainly the least, these two hags are no different from the slanderous, verbally abusive faculty. Ironically, it's absurd the supposed logical (Biology) teacher and the supposed cultured (Spanish) instructor would capitulate to harassing a lone student due to baseless rumors.

It just goes to show all the education, diplomas and achievements are inconsequential against these shitty excuses for lecturers and their disgusting habits of verbal abuse, mob mentality, and most importantly: *toxic femininity.*

Mrs. Samantha and Ms. Bonny were both pleasant people at first during Freshman year. I found the former's biology's class informative and was somewhat interested learning Spanish from the latter. However, as expected, both became hostile, histrionic, bitter, liars later, towards me, over the slander that permeated shithole SJHS.

In reference to Mrs. Samantha, I noticed her "slight heel turn" towards the snakes' lies in one, particular event. It occurred one day, during the early September weeks of Freshman year, biology class. All the snakes were talking amongst each other while I was reading a book, waiting for class to begin.

A snake asked Mrs. Samantha a question concerning *"a student who was a loner."* Mrs. Samantha, answered loudly to the whole class:

"If a student goes out of their way to avoid others, it gives the impression of arrogance."

I could tell that question and answer was directed at me (backhandedly), but I found it to be weird at the time. At least her answer wasn't out of malice, but most likely ignorance.

I didn't understand how avoidance is equivalent to arrogance. Would any sensible people associate with strangers in a dark alley? No. Most individuals would avoid them, which was how I viewed the snakes. Also at that time, the snakes were already slandering and hurling insults at me, so it was pointless to befriend people with no morals.

Personally, **I despise loud and vulgar people,** which the snakes embodied, *so why couldn't they understand that not everyone tolerates their behavior?* From my perspective, it's practically narcissistic of the snakes to expect everyone to acclimate and assimilate to their loud, barbaric, degenerate behavior.

Throughout my life, I witnessed family members ingratiate themselves into the wrong crowd. Just to avoid isolation. As a teen and even now as an adult, I refused to compromise my morals for association, which was another reason I avoided the snakes.

At that moment, after Mrs. Samantha made her "grand speech" about loners. *I mistakenly trusted the adult of the room, to figure out another reason for my avoidance.* In hindsight, how would she have responded if I questioned her fallacious logic, like this:

"If a student who has experienced bullying from both students and teachers in jr. high, is now being harassed again in high school, would you blame that student for their avoidance of people?"

For the rest of the year, Mrs. Samantha wasn't outwardly slanderous. However, I couldn't completely trust her, since the rest of the sleazy pedagogues had already begun to castigate me.

Regarding Mrs. Bonny, her façade of a posh, well-mannered Caribbean was beginning to crack by Freshman year, from my perspective. Even though she politely greeted me every morning, predictably, she quietly hurled the same insult about my body. Every time, every morning in Spanish class, Beldam Bonny uttered:

"No one wants to see that," repeating the same, spineless falsity as the pedo-pedagogues.

Despite her beratement towards me, I earned a high grade in her class.

I had to deal with her again by Junior year for Spanish III. As expected, she was slowly showcasing her bitter broad hostility, like a mask cracking into pieces, unveiling a decrepit, decomposing, husk of person, with sludge for a soul. Once again, I achieved high marks on the weekly tests.

Then, out of nowhere, on a spring afternoon, after distributing the class's weekly quiz results, Beldam Bonny weirdly insulted my intelligence…

"Don't let it go to your head. You always study at the last minute." The crone discreetly muttered.

Honestly, I didn't understand what the "burnt beldam" was furious about. Was she expecting me to fail? Was she offended that I found her language easy to learn? I like to think she was looking for any excuse to defame and berate me.

In the same season, burnt beldam Bonny openly humiliated me twice. Thus, her "mask" slipped. The first incident happened when the snakes and I were dispersed into smaller groups for classwork. After the work was done, the two other snakes were chatting among themselves, and I decided to peruse a book as usual, when left to my own devices.

Out of nowhere, the belligerent burnt beldam, yelled the *most puerile* insult of me to the whole class:

"Look, she's reading! All she does is read!"

Around half of the snakes laughed in unison. The loudest ones were those **who read at a snail's pace, aloud**, when given the task in English class. I chose to ignore the matchstick beldam's harassment, to deprive her of a reaction.

The second incident happened around April, when I had to move to the last row. While others may see these two events as "teasing", me recognizing the harassment patterns from the ***"charred up crone"*** demonstrates her immaturity from emulating the snakes' slanderous behavior. I like to believe her mental faculties were declining.

By the time Senior year rolled around, part of me anticipated Mrs. Samantha to begin verbally abusing me. After all, the other lying pedagogues did it more brazenly.

I was interested in learning psychology, so I had to take the only elective class taught by her. By mid-spring, Moby Samantha began to show her resentment towards me.

On a mid-spring day, she brought in her two toddler daughters to demonstrate how children have underdeveloped brains and can't comprehend the concept of mass.

The class was informative, as usual. However, at the end, as I walked pass Moby Samantha and her daughters, she made a hostile glare at me and mouthed *"What the hell?"* silently. While doing so, she grabbed her two daughters. I was mostly confused but realized that Moby Samantha assumed I was trying to seduce her. Just like the other perverted, religious instructors who blamed my buxom body.

On the other hand, the dim-witted Moby Samantha didn't persecute **ANY** of the other snakes that showed off their lower back and borderline butt cracks, near her children. ***What an idiotic whale.***

To culminate Moby Samantha's unwarranted mistreatment towards me. Her last hostile act ensued on the final day of psychology class.

It was a scorching, hot mid-May afternoon. Moby Samantha commenced a "final speech" to the class. She traipsed her whale tail for legs, down the aisle of desks:

"All of you may grow out into beautiful women…" As she gently spoke.

While approaching the last row, where I was, I started having a slight anxiety attack. My heart began to beat quickly.

Moby Samantha reached the end of the aisle and turned towards the right. Suddenly, she swiftly turned around:

"BUT I DON'T KNOW WHAT YOU'LL END UP AS!"

The unhinged whale, Moby Samantha, was referring to me, since she screamed in my direction. In addition, I noticed her facing the same way towards my desk from my peripheral vision. The rest of the snakes were oddly silent.

As mentioned before, I have a knack for evoking people's hatred of me without doing anything to them. Therefore, Moby Samantha's meltdown or whatever, was the result of her falsely accusing me, based on empty rumors and no evidence.

I didn't have Beldam Bonny the zombie for my final year. However, she finally unveiled her corrupt nature to me in the month of mid-May.

I was heading to the library on the second floor, in the afternoon during a break period and I was parched too.

There was a short water fountain in the hallway of the same floor, so I decided to use that instead of heading to the lunchroom. I felt awkward using the short fountain by having to bend over as a tall person.

While drinking from the fountain, burnt bedlam Bonny and the Spanish II instructor, Mrs. Z walked past me. The walking matchstick Bonny clicked her tongue in a sign of disgust while doing so. When I finally finished, she and Mrs. Z were ahead of me and near the library, she turned her head and yelled:

"FAGGOT!"

Like a demented crone.

At that moment, I witnessed the demon lurking behind the charred cunt's mask.

Regarding both worthless bitches, I found their random shouting a form of *menopausal hysteria,* coupled with unearned self-righteousness, audaciousness and a low IQ to assume that they know everything about me from fictional rumors. If there's one thing **shithole SJHS** has, is high number of unhinged broads.

Conclusion

I feel like I've been conned from society after I graduated from Shithole St. Joseph's. It's highly depressing that the false persecution, dehumanization and harassment of the student body and pedagogy that inflicted upon me was hand-waived and obscured for more funding, and prestige for the former. At the very least, with multiple corrupt schools like Shithole SJHS, I'm elated that parents all around the country have initiated to homeschool their children. After reflecting through my tenure, it's evident that American society, maybe the whole world, has become low-trust and abusive.

One lesson I obtained from those pedos and sadists at shithole SJHS: ***"I won't be like them."*** Experiencing their slander, verbal abuse and humiliation resulted in me becoming more pious. I realized how rampant sin and malevolence perpetuate and subsist in "religious" institutions. Also, I began to doubt the holiness of the Catholic Church but remained loyal to God.

With all the pain I suffered from SJHS, I witnessed how liars and hypocrites are abounding and in power. Equivocal to Hollywood's *casting couch* and truly undeserving of respect. Likewise, this reasoning is why the verse:

"Love not the world, neither the things that are in the world. If any man loves the world, the love of the Father is not in him," **(1 John 2:15 KJV)**

Resonates with me because I'll always refuse to engage with evil people and malicious actions. It's inconsequential to me if an individual or group retains exclusive social status, wealth, or power in society when their behaviors, personalities and character are malicious. I prefer to stay true to my morals and integrity. Something the SJHS chimos will never possess.

As a teenager, I always pontificated,

How do evil people like them live with themselves?

Are their consciousnesses seared?

Do they even have souls?

Honestly, it's pointless to reason with evil, especially in the soulless, disingenuous chimos of shithole SJHS.

A second lesson I've understood: ***"is to rebel against corrupt authorities."*** If an authoritative figure itself is malicious, then I won't respect him/her nor the power they were given. In the case of the sleazy, slanderous instructors of shithole SJHS, they are, at the utmost: *reprobates of the highest order*. Regardless of how many times, they attend church, or openly praise God, only destruction, suffering and hell await hypocrites like them, just like the pain they inflicted in their miserable lives. As stated in the New Testament:

"Not everyone that saith unto me, Lord, Lord, shall enter into the kingdom of heaven; but he that doeth the will of my Father which is in heaven" **(Matt.7:21 KJV).**

Bolstering that verse, are the continuous scandals from the Catholic Church. Considering I'm not the only victim who was abused, it won't be long before society castigates the Vatican, regardless of all pomp, praise and authority it exerts in the media and throughout the world. Ask yourself, *dear reader*, **Would God condone child abusers in his house?**

In addition to the continuous abuse and bullying from students and/or teachers, that persists even in public schools, I believe additional cameras should be installed to protect students. Also, the public, especially instructors and students, should be educated on neurodivergence so not to misjudge or assume malice from neurodivergent students.

Since rapists' parade in Hollywood, murderers are paid in hospitals and pedophiles abuse the youth. I've learned it's imperative to stomp out evil, with no mercy, **with your own hands**, as institutional corruption is prevalent in society, which is one of my objectives for writing this memoir.

Regarding the mistreatment I underwent at shithole SJHS, what better way to eradicate my tormentors and slanderers than to expose the truth of their abuse towards me? Furthermore, *"evil prevails when good people do nothing."* Which compelled me even further to document my tenure at SJHS. It's inconsequential of *"how long ago"* my abuse was. It is more valuable to notice and rebel against abusive authorities in power. Knowing their disgusting nature that I'm apprised of, this memoir of mine is equivalent to showing a crucifix, to demons like them.

Epilogue

I won't deny that I don't have any regrets from surviving shithole SJHS. I wished I were more assertive. I wished I gave all those derelict teachers a black eye...or a bullet (just joking). Also, I wished I wasn't so negative, morose, and hopeless about my harassment. Being bullied from Jr. High to High school and even college gave me the impression that I'll always be harassed by my body type, and my gentle nature, even if I did transfer. More importantly, I wished I considered home schooling after surviving sexual harassment and slander during Jr. high.

After all, should a bullied, depressed teen be retraumatized in a poor environment of pedo-adjacent, verbally abusive instructors and duplicitous, ghetto, whorish trollops for students? Ultimately, it's pointless to keep blaming myself for the past, nor can I just "*move on*" with my life, knowing these filthy slanderers, sadists and harassers walk the earth, unscathed.

In my adulthood, within my small, lone, apartment I suffer from insomnia, my chest tightens, my heart beats rapidly, and I have bouts of anger where I accidently punch furniture as the disgusting memories of being unfairly castigated by the perverted teachers flow through my mind. With these horrible, PTSD-like symptoms I find myself walking back and forth through my apartment, attempting to calm myself down, with prayer. However, with these symptoms and my unbridled righteous indignation, my soul is screaming to reveal the monsters that enjoyed falsely persecuting and slandering me. I may have been a victim back then, but now I'm not helpless nor weak to expose the evil I experienced.

The most effective treatment for **the nightmares, the flashbacks, anxiety and meltdowns** I still suffer to this day is to unveil the maliciousness of these vile pigs. Logically, this is the most Christian, penultimate response to unwavering, relentless, carnal, ostensible, evil (**Matthew 5:11 KJV**), that stoicism, modern therapy or the *"court system"* could never remedy, in my opinion. I'm aware God equalizes vengeance towards the wicked (**Romans 12:19 KJV**) but he wouldn't admonish me for exposing these skin-walking, slanderous, sanctimonious demons who fail to follow his word.

Every day, my entire being yearns for justice against the verbal and psychological abuse I endured. The authorities were always ineffective in my youth, so therefore, exposing the truth of my abuse and harassment will finally put my mind at ease and soul to rest. Personally, I feel as though a great weight has been lifted off my shoulders as I write and unveil the tragedies I've endured. ***However, this is just the beginning of the expose' of all the evil that I've endured.***

Not only am I pouring my soul, tears and righteous indignation into this memoir, but I am also writing this for the youths who are castigated for being neurodivergent, who couldn't conform to societal norms. Individuals like you are profoundly unique, and society is unable to or slowly embrace you. Please don't ever hate yourself for you are the most prominent symbol of uniqueness.

I'm scribing this for the young females who physically mature early. There is nothing wrong with your body, or your mind. You will always be a human being above all else**, not an object to be sexualized.** I implore you to avoid and expose perverts who harass and treat you like garbage over something you can't control.

Finally, to all the youths reading this, social status and hierarchy doesn't mean ***jack shit*** when a teacher, counselor or even a principal mistreats you, permits evil and lacks morals. ***Don't respect those who won't respect you.***

To all the incompetent, slanderers and predatory "pedagogy" of (the former) St. Joseph's High School that were featured here, I intend to notify that society is cognizant of your abuse. Your achievements are ***"dirty rags"*** (**Isaiah 64:6-7 KJV**) regarding your repugnant behavior. Plus, your expertise in youth education is insignificant, while you take delight in slandering, sexually harassing a neurodivergent, traumatized minor for her body. Part of me used to ponder how do you scum live with yourselves, But it's pointless to reason with sentient dung. You will pay for your ***deformation, sadism, and pride.***

Therefore, here is the **absolute truth from me**…

I was never attracted to you, perverts.

I never wanted your attention.

You're beyond idiotic for assuming a buxom student was tempting you,

by...keeping to herself or walking past you.

You permitted the other female students of showing off their lower stomachs and wearing skirts above their knees. Like the hypocrites and perverts, you are.

You incompetent instructors lied to my face, slandered me behind my back, and ridiculed me for your own enjoyment.

You sexualized a black, female minor for her body, while bloviating about accepting diversity.

You were too cowardly, envious, and sleazy to ascertain the truth about me.

You were too immature, sadistic, and worthless to tolerate and respect a neurodivergent student.

You are useless, imbecilic, slaves to the government that acclimate to Catholic school minor abuse.

If you pedos didn't slander and sexually harass me, you wouldn't be in this situation.

Before you enter the gates of hell, your life on Earth won't be pleasant from here on out.

The following are my final words to you.

Your treatment towards me showed how ugly you are...

Now, I'll show the world how abhorrent you really are.

Your friends will ostracize you.

Your family will abhor you.

Your partner will never love you again.

Your descendants will be ashamed of you.

You've already disgraced your ancestors.

Your neighbors will disgustingly avoid you.

Society will disregard you with scorn and ridicule.

The media will ignore your lies and excuses.

The internet will never forgive or forget you.

Your abuse will be remembered worldwide.

Your final years will be filled with torment.

Even after death...

The "Heaven" you claim to worship will oust you like trash.

The "Hell" you wanted to circumvent, will embrace and torture you.

Your worthless corpse or ashes will only be reminded of your...

Crimes, like the vile scum you all are.

Dedications

*I dedicate this memoir to the **Holy Trinity: God the Father**, **Jesus the Son** and to the **Holy Spirit**. You all guided me to believe in myself and in my innocence as I experienced false persecution, slander, and sexual harassment even to this day. You also imbued me with the courage to expose evil.*

To my father, thank you for advising me on how to be assertive, especially with myself. To my late mother, I thank you for instructing me to stand up for myself, choose my battles, and to show no mercy against those who would wrong me.

Finally, I dedicate this memoir to all the readers who read about my strife and the hell that I underwent.

www.ingramcontent.com/pod-product-compliance
Lightning Source LLC
Chambersburg PA
CBHW071708040426
42446CB00011B/1965